LIFE LESSONS

On Becoming a Young Man

Written By

Stanley Ash, B.A., M.Ed.

Copyright© 2011 by Stanley Ash

All rights reserved.

This publication is designed to provide competent and reliable inspirational information regarding subject matters covered. No part of this publication may be reproduced, stored in a retrieval system, or transmitted, in any form or by any means, electronic, mechanical, photocopying, recording, or otherwise, without the prior written permission of the author, except for brief quotes used in review.

Library of Congress Cataloguing-in-Publication Data has been applied for

Publishing Consultant:

Deborah M. Smart

http://www.gladstonepublishing.com

Printed in United States

ISBN-13: 978-1-928681-23-6

ISBN-10: 1-928681-23-9

Imprint: Gladstone Publishing Services

Dedication

It is with the deepest gratitude that I pay tribute to the following individuals and groups for their continuous support in aiding in the completion of this written endeavor. Skip and Gayle Enlow who critically critiqued my earliest writings. Brother Faheem and his wife Debbie who unknowingly guided me through this seemingly endless process for the past year. Cousin Louise whose unending love for the family has sustained me in this task by keeping me focused. Ethel Boyd Owens who listened very attentively as I repeatedly rewrote almost everything that I thought was perfect. My family for allotting me the uninterrupted time to complete this project. The various churches that agreed to listen to these vignettes and offer their critiques. And finally it would be negligent of me to forget to mention Doane College.

It was Doane College over 40 years ago that took a chance on a young very worldly African American teen. It was Doane that saw in me someone worthwhile and in need of getting a second chance to get a college education. Those in charge of making admission decisions must have seen something in me and believed that perhaps I could flourish in rural Nebraska. And it is with that four years served at Doane where I was able to fine tune my abilities as a student. It was there in the rural confines of "little" Doane College where I was able to develop into a teacher, an administrator and now perhaps a writer.

Introduction

The author, Stanley Ash, BA, M.Ed., was born in the Bronx, New York City. He is a product of the New York City public school system. Throughout his years in the New York City public and growing up in the Bronx he grappled with getting a decent education. This struggle to get an education was by no means strictly due to the short comings of the system, but perhaps was to a greater extent attributed to his low income urban neighborhood. This was a neighborhood that did not stress the academics. An area where a good education was never really emphasized, admired, or sought after. It could even be said that those of us who were fortunate enough to get an education was pretty much the result of the life lessons that we learned from our neighborhood, friends, and family. This book is dedicated to those…**Life Lessons**. It is the author's intent that by sharing some of his life lessons that you the reader can indeed reap some of the same benefits that he received from living them.

Table of Contents

Chapter One – Prayerfully	1
Legacy of an Uneducated Man	2
Ruler of the Roost	13
Monroe Ash: A Parent for All Seasons	18
A Holiday Treat	24
Chapter Two – Few Things Can Compare	31
Leaving Heaven	34
Early Manhood Training – Physical	43
Early Manhood Training – Philosophical	49
A Time for Never Again	55
Chapter Three – A Thought	61
Fear of the Unknown	62
Walk This Way	68
The Garment District	72
Too Much Mouth	80
Chapter Four – The Brother's Brother	86
Brotherly Inspiration	88
The Art of Attraction	94

Book of James	100
Thin Line Between Love and Hate	109
Chapter Five – Trash Talking	**115**
The Story of David	117
Obtaining Friendship	125
The Beginning of the End	132
Minford Place	138
The Chosen One	146

Chapter One
Prayerfully

His words are not that uncommon. Many have uttered these words before,

But still they have a degree of unfamiliarity.

His words only come during a major crisis.

His words are mostly stated in the privacy of his bedroom.

His words are said as he drops to his knees.

His words are personal.

He is…**prayerfully focused**.

He makes no pretense that his words are the most important, for he is not certain.

He connects long phrases in hopes that it will be understood.

He expresses a long list of wishes and desires never feeling that he has to repeat himself.

He sometimes sweats profusely as if to accentuate the importance of his words.

He takes sole proprietorship of his statements.

He is worried.

He is fearful.

He closes with "Amen".

He is a…**prayerful man**.

Legacy of an Uneducated Man

In spite of what some may say, or believe, we don't achieve on our own. Quotes such as "I am a self-made man" or "I did it all by myself." It is my contention that we are indeed somewhat off track if we believe this. Consider the following: If we truly are self made men, then our parents, friends, family, and ancestors played no part whatsoever. We must have been born, lived, accomplished monumental tasks, set world records, over-came insurmountable obstacles, all of this was done purely by the individual's own self initiative.

Allow me the opportunity to say that my father played a major role in me being the person that I am today. My father, the uneducated, educated man.

Through him I learned and was taught both directly and indirectly. Directly he taught through the power of the belt. He didn't negotiate. He didn't compromise. His in-famous quotes still command my attention after his demise. "I have a one track mind"…"It's going to be me and you." Be-cause of a difficult work schedule, which consisted of him working the graveyard shift, he was unable to have the time to spend with his kids that some parents might have today.

Indirectly I learned deeply philosophical lessons from this man who never studied philosophy. I learned that a man should not smile without a reason. It seems like most of my earlier years growing up he never smiled. He never smiled if he had to come to school for one of his children. He never smiled when he told my brothers and I that it was time to go to school. It seemed like he never would smile.

Unbelievably he did smile if someone told him something humorous...which was rare. Through him I learned how to be innovative. Since he worked at nights he couldn't institute the type of discipline that he felt that his four sons and one daughter needed. Subsequently he created "judgment day." His judgment day occurred every Saturday morning. At that time he would issue some very decisive decisions for his children who had broken the house rules during the course of the week. These judgments would be the direct result of what my mother reported to him on Saturday morning. His judgments would most likely result in either issuing out an allowance for those who obeyed the rules or a marathon beating for those who broke the house rules...he did not negotiate.

Although he only stood 5'3" tall he commanded the respect of all of his children. In my father's house there was no democracy. He was the commander-in-chief, the CEO, the president, and the Lord and master. So when he said that you were going to get an education he meant it. He didn't negotiate. Some of the things that he said I did not like nor did I appreciate. On one occasion when I arrived home with some Algebra homework that I did not understand, I complained that I couldn't do the homework. What he told me on that occasion helped me to truly understand life. For it was on that occasion that he told me...you will sit there until you understand that Algebra! So that night while I sat there with my mother overseeing my efforts to get this done I had an epiphany. I began to sniffle as tears crept down my face. I believed that I could solicit some sympathy from my mother for my predicament. It was at that moment that I remembered that tears didn't work in my father's house. Shortly thereafter I concluded that I had to seek out another solution. The next day I decided that my best hope was to stay after school and get help from one of my teachers.

Much of my time during my formative years was spent remembering the directives of my father. With this in mind I never had a problem being focused in school. Both James and Sherman had repeatedly warned me about what happens when "Daddy" came to school. One of the many accounts of my father coming to school came from Sherman. According to him he had informed my father that a teacher was "picking" on him. Having said this, my brother was sure that my father would come to school and "straighten this teacher out." Unfortunately for Sherman that is not how it worked out. After hearing what the teacher had to say my father looked across at Sherman and said, "It's going to be me and you." This particular statement generally meant that you were slated to receive a severe beating come Saturday. With this revelation from my brother, who I knew possessed great wisdom; I never did anything to cause a teacher to send for my father (my mother allowed my father to handle any school problems).

Another reason for my not wanting my father to come to school to see my teachers was self-hatred. My father, as I learned from other kids, was too dark. Frequently they would make jokes about dark skinned Negroes. The unfortunate part was that the kids saying those things were from my own culture. Self-hate was prevalent during the mid-60s. At one point I became quite self-conscious about skin complexion. But somehow through it all regardless of concerns about complexion I continued to strive to get an education.

The Last Lesson

Throughout high school I had a great time. I studied just enough so that my father wouldn't have to go to school, but I never set any records for academic success. I studied very hard trying to get around things as opposed to doing it the right way. I made it my business to attend as many social events that my high school offered. I sought to become the proverbial party animal. If there was a party I knew about it. It became my specialty to know most of the students in the school that were leaders or well known. And I wanted them to know me.

Unfortunately for me I turned 18 during the War in Vietnam. At that time there existed in this country something called the draft. And according to the draft at 18 you were expected to register for the armed forces. Shortly after I turned 18 I received my "1A" classification and was directed to register for the armed forces at my local recruitment office. For some unknown reason the recruitment office didn't seem to care that I was a "social force" within my high school. They could care less that I could dance, that I knew where the parties were, or how to get out of doing work in high school.

With my new classification I immediately went to my guidance counselor for some assistance, or way out of going into the service. During the Vietnam War Black men were dying at an alarming rate and I didn't want to become one of those statistics. After talking to the counselor I soon realized that although I ranked in the top ten socially, in the area of academics I fell within the bottom 10% of the senior class. It was very difficult being both a social climber and an academic student. Fortunately for me my counselor found out that there was a school who would even accept a student like me.

It was my intention to attend school to avoid having to participate in the draft at that time. During the draft if a student was in college usually they did not draft you into the armed forces. The school that my counselor found for me was 1300 miles away in the state of Nebraska. Even then it was amazing the lengths that a young man would go to in order to avoid putting himself in harm's way. For some strange reason I didn't care where it was I just knew that I did not want to go into the armed forces.

With my acceptance into Doane College I just knew that I had truly accomplished something that other students like myself would kill for, an opportunity to go to college after doing so very little in high school. Somehow, I had once again gotten over. But little did I realize that man, my father, the "uneducated educated man," would once again teach me a most valuable lesson about life.

On the morning that I was to leave for the airport there was great excitement in the Ash household. For some reason, that I don't recall only my father accompanied me to the airport. Being a poor family from the projects and living in New York City we had no car. So, we took a taxicab to the airport. Like most young folks about to go off to new challenges I was very excited until my father gave his words of wisdom. He presented me with an airline ticket which didn't have on it what I was looking for...it was a **ONE WAY TICKET**. In this one simple act my father had said so much without uttering one single word. In this one instance I came to realize the meaning of non verbal communication.

It was in this very strange and unusual act of the disbursement of the ticket that I came to realize several things. A son should never question his father. Although I think I understood the significance of the one way ticket I dared not ask. In addition I realized that as men sometimes we don't know something, but we don't ask for fear of putting our ignorance on public display. Suppose I was wrong in my assessment of the situation...why risk it? And finally as men we do a lot of things without any verbal questions and believe that all men should understand what we are trying to say. After all, what man would dare to say I don't understand what you mean? Where is the round trip ticket?

Ruler of the Roost

Over the years I have come to realize that every household has to have a ruler of the roost. It is almost imperative that someone becomes the "go to person", the "leader of the pack", the one that everyone views as the "head honcho." In the Ash household this person was Monroe Ash, my father. He was clearly an example of not judging a book by its cover. Monroe only stood about 5'3" tall and weighed about 155 lbs., but he was the king of his domain.

The entire structure of the house came from this southern Negro from Georgia. In letting it be known that this was his home my father never shirked his responsibility. From the beginning of the day to the end of the evening he was the HNIC (Head Negro in Charge). It was within this realm that no one challenged my father, not my brothers, sister, and certainly not me. Although this structural arrangement may have seemed somewhat archaic it worked for us.

Life according to Monroe was very restrictive which worked for him and in turn was supposed to work for us. My father felt that all of us needed to have a certain time to be in from the streets. Typically this time centered on the time when it got dark. In his infinite wisdom he could envision that there wasn't anything worthwhile going on after dark on the streets...so we should be in the house. In addition Monroe felt that all of us should have chores to do. With this in mind he assigned duties for all of us to do in the house. The distribution of these chores he felt would add to the better day to day functioning of the household. Furthermore he set up a very rigid code of discipline for the Ash family. His word was law. And when the word was given it became the law. Far be it for us to question whether or not he was assuming god like powers. After all he wasn't god...was he?

There was a time when we could never really understand the need for all of this structure. For all of what we didn't under-stand today's parents can truly appreciate. Even though these things took place over forty years ago they still all make sense today. For instance, all of us had a certain time to be in. By utilizing this simple procedure fewer children would possibly be snatched up by strangers, get involved in questionable activities, or generally get into things that they shouldn't. The idea of having chores to do indirectly taught us responsibility and/or gave us the ability to complete a task or suffer the consequences of not finishing. And, what about the roles of parents vs. children? In my father's mind there existed only two worlds. One specifically for children and the other relegated to adults. The adult world was not rated X it simply meant that certain things were meant for adults to take part in because they maintained an adult perspective…not the perspective of a child. And everything else was allotted to the children for their participation. These two worlds were never allowed to coexist in the same time frame.

Another consideration from the world according to Monroe was that he appreciated credentials but recognized experience. My father saw credentials for what they were worth a status awarded to a person for having achieved a certain status. But he also saw the value of a lifetime of experience which often came with no paper. I think he realized there were a lot of educated fools pretty much everywhere. Monroe appreciated people who could think on their feet a lot more than those who had to refer to their title to establish some type of credibility. In other words someone who had to constantly remind you that they were the "head negro in charge." It would seem that we still have some of the same types today.

Monroe Ash:
A Parent for all Seasons

Monroe Ash the patriarch of the Ash family was unique for the time in which he lived and probably would have been unique for today's time too. There were several qualities of his that were most memorable. One of these was his steadfastness in main-taining his family. My father took great pride in knowing that he was able to provide for his family in spite of what was going on all around him. He would often speak with great enthusiasm about being able to have meat at every meal. This was important to him. For a black man who didn't make money most of his life to be able to put meat on the table every night was tantamount to being Houdini.

Another endearing quality was his ability and willingness to work. There were few if any times that my father did not go to work. He didn't believe in taking time off from work. He would frequently remind my brothers and me about the importance of having and keeping a job. "I don't want to have no bum living in my house." He was determined that none of his sons would be a bum. He abhorred the idea of one of us bringing this type of dishonor to the Ash household. Over the years we began to adhere to this belief also. The Ash men always managed to maintain some type of legal employment; to do otherwise was unthinkable.

A third ability that my father possessed was that of being able to impose his will on his children. Even when he was not around I think that all of us felt his presence constantly.

Whenever we considered doing something wrong we either conjured up images of his ever present accusing index finger pointing directly at us thus causing us to think twice about what we were about to do. It seemed to be a consistent reminder that come Saturday, he would be waiting to inflict his form of discipline on us if we didn't stay the course and do the right thing. For us our father, Monroe, was almost God-like. He was omnipresent in everything that we did or thought about doing.

There were times when I felt that my father would have made an excellent practitioner of the martial arts. This conclusion was arrived at after realizing that all of the time when our father metered out discipline, he practiced tremendous control much like a martial arts master. On Saturday morning when we received our beatings he always maintained control. In these encounters he would call us in the room one by one and ask our mother had we done our chores. If our chores were done in accordance with his mandate we would receive an allowance. If for some reason we did not perform our assigned duties we incurred his judgment, thus the name for Saturday became "Judgment Day."

Along with some of these notable qualities he still had some others. My father always gave us the impression that he was fearless. One reason we felt this about him was because of where he worked at. For many years our father worked in a 16 story office building at night by himself. It was his job to clean that whole building by himself at night. On several occasions he showed me how he went about his task of cleaning the building at night. He systematically went from floor to floor emptying the trash cans, mopping the floors, etc. The whole time as he went about his task there were all kinds of strange sounds coming from the building most of which I couldn't account for. None of these noises appeared to bother him. He simply continued to do his task of cleaning the building.

Being in my father's presence there were many lessons to be learned. One of the things that I learned indirectly was that size didn't really matter. At the time I really didn't know too many men smaller than my father. Although he only stood 5'3" tall and weighed about 155 he never exhibited any fear of anyone. He neither showed nor expressed fear of anyone that walked this planet. This I learned by walking with him and watching him operate. Most of my young life he consistently walked fast. He would never stop to engage in conversation with any stranger on the street. "Excuse me sir, you have any change?" My father would say "no" and never break stride. Whenever I walked with him he always appeared to be in a hurry. For a small man he walked very fast.

Something else that I attribute to learning from my father indirectly was the complexion issue in the black community; the conflict between dark skinned blacks and the much lighter version of black folks. There were those situations when I looked at my father differently because of his very dark complexioned skin. Some in the neighborhood viewed my father as being "purple." This was a designation typically given to black folks who were very dark. For my father none of this seemed to matter. He knew who he was and what he was about. He was about Black pride before it became popular to do so. To me he indeed set the standard for all of his children to follow. He was a parent for all situations and circumstances. In other words, a parent for all seasons.

Holiday Treat

For some strange reason my memory fails me in terms of exactly when it started, but I do know the parts of the ritual. It started with the advent of the holiday season which included either Christmas or New Years. Both of these days held great significance in our household. Perhaps it was the time of the year; the closing out of one year and the beginning of another. That having been said I cannot remember a time when my father did not have to work on either Christmas or New Years. Never did he receive both days off.

The ritual involved the preparation of the holiday meal. The major concern in the preparation of the meal was to make sure that my father received a hot meal...at his place of employment. Unfortunately for the Ash family this always proved to be a major undertaking. The main reason for the difficulty was that while living in New York City we were a carless family. We traveled everywhere by means of public transportation. This included to work, school, shopping, etc. For us this seemed to be the natural way of doing things. You either rode the bus or the subway (train). So getting a hot dinner to my father at his job required a lot of preparation, both mental and physical. For my mother it appeared to be easy, but for us it was like taking a major trip that could very easily turn into a 3-4 hour journey.

The preparation of the food was the easy part. My mother merely prepared my father's dinner with the regular family meal. It was after we had eaten when the journey would begin. We had to pack everything up.

This typically included turkey, ham, giblets, gravy, macaroni & cheese, rice, collards, string beans, sweet potatoes, and of course corn bread. My father, as well the rest of us, loved corn bread. Along with this meal we had to bring an assortment of pot holders, kitchen towels, napkins, silverware, and some type of beverage. In addition my mother included a pot. The purpose of this pot was to put water in it to heat the food. During those times they didn't have hot plates or anything similar to it or we just couldn't afford to buy one.

The journey to my father's job took about 45 minutes to an hour. We had to ride the subway there and then walk a few blocks when we got off of the train. All along we carried these two shopping bags loaded with this freshly prepared holiday meal in it. This indeed was a meal prepared for a "king." After all, how many wives would even consider doing such a thing? Why not do like contemporary wives, prepare that meal, leave it in the refrigerator for him when he got home, and tell him to warm it up himself? For some unbeknownst reason this was how my mother felt that it was supposed to done. In other words make a man feel like he was a king and be prepared to serve him or just do more than the next woman.

When we arrived he very quickly ushered us into a huge office building of about sixteen floors. My father was the only employee on the premises other than the night watchman. Once inside we would go to a room where my father usually ate his dinner...by himself. Although this bothered me, none of this seemed to bother him. In my mind I couldn't fathom the idea of being in a building that large and pretty much by myself. But according to my father it didn't bother him. It was in this message I came to another revelation about manhood. A man will take on all soughts of odd or unusual situations in order to provide for his family...without complaining. I think if he didn't have a family he might have viewed the job differently.

Looking back I can't help but feel that the meal satisfied both the body and the soul. For it was during the few hours that my mother and I spent there that I saw a joy seldom seen in my father before. He genuinely seemed happy. I would suppose that having a family that thought that much of him to come all of the way down town on a holiday evening to have dinner with him furthered his belief that there was truly love and respect for him in his family unit. For once my father even seemed kind of jovial…I suppose.

While there my father typically revealed a lot about what he did in the building. Having heard most of this before I quickly realized it was my obligation to listen once again. Besides on each occasion I learned something else either directly or indirectly. I soon realized that in spite of his lack of a formal education my father had access to a lot of knowledge. This too was a reminder to me that having a live-in father allowed me access to a lot of worldly knowledge. I've often wondered where would I be now in my life had I not had this opportunity. Experiencing this part I've gotten a better understanding of why our young African American males who don't have fathers at home often struggle with their life choices. The good thing was that he didn't mind dispensing this information especially to someone like me who was willing to listen.

Upon us making our exit from the building my father assured us that he would see us in the morning. We left just as quietly and quickly as we had come. The trip home always seemed much shorter than the trip there. It probably had something to do with my quietly trying to disseminate all of the information my father had given me. The train ride gave me the opportunity to do a great deal of reflecting. Sometimes I would ride the whole time without saying a word. I had a lot to digest. My father's words always left me doing a lot of contemplating. A lot of contemplating!!

Chapter Two

Few Things Can Compare

As men we sometimes rejoice in knowing that very few men
are blessed to have sons.
After all there are a higher percentage of females born
then males each year.
So, as a result we tend to bask in the glory of being one
of those chosen to have a son.
Few things can compare with this experience.

In the beginning with all their energy it seems like
they would live forever;
But quickly we learn that forever can be very subjective.
As a father you do your best to instill within that son all that you
think he will need to know to survive this life, but it never
seems to be enough.
You show him all of what you know and all of what you learned
with the hope that it will insulate him from life's many pitfalls.
Few things can compare with the inquiring mind of a son.

As time passes a father can bear witness to the fruits of his
efforts.
The son becomes a man and has a chance to test
all of what he has learned.
There will be times when he will stumble, but the father
must merely watch.

There will be times when the father can see a mistake that the
son may be about to make,
But he must be allowed to experience the lessons of life.
If he has learned his lessons well he will realize that the fork in
the road is not an obstacle, but a choice to be made.
Few things can compare with evolving into a man.

As a father we try to teach that very few things
are permanent on this planet.
So we urge our sons to enjoy those things while you have
them.
As a father we try to explain the yin and yang of the universe,
the existence of opposites;
As a father we tell our son that for every no that you hear
that there is a yes waiting down the road
As a father we inform our son that for every hardship that he
may experience that happiness looms on the horizon.
As a father we remind our son that as the Sun rises,
one day it must certainly set.
Few things can compare with the beginning of one day
and the ending of another.

As fathers we sometimes feel that with the setting of the Sun
the day has ended.
It is at this time that the father has to go back to his roots
and become a student again and speak to his FATHER (creator).
It is at this time that the father realizes that he has had
his blessing for a number of years.
It is at this time that the father sees that he has had the benefit

of viewing the development of a man.
It is at this time that the father is reminded that he was blessed.
Few things can compare with the loss of a son.

As a father I offer thanks to the Creator (God) for allowing me to have my son for so long.
As a father I appreciate the opportunity to share my humble wisdom
with him during his brief stay on this planet.
Few things can compare with being blessed with a son even for a short period of time.

Leaving Heaven

There was a time in the very distant past when it would have seemed unimaginable to consider leaving the projects. For those who never lived there perhaps they just don't get it. The "projects" was a world within a world. As a young person I could only see the benefits of dwelling there and none of the pitfalls.

The projects for me offered numerous benefits that seemingly didn't exist anywhere else. To begin with it offered an almost insurmountable amount of security. Once you were in the "walls" of the limited amount of grass that surrounded the several high-rise buildings you were safe. You were safe from pretty much everything that plagued the rest of the civilized world. As residents of our project, "the Forest Projects," we loved the comraderieship that came with being project dwellers. We were isolated from gang warfare, robberies, murder, rape, etc. This was our heaven or so we thought.

Being a project dweller the concept of fear seemed so foreign to most of those that I considered my friends. In the summer it was not unusual to stay out until two or three o'clock in the morning playing games outside. This is not to say that there were not minor skirmishes within the confines of the projects. The difference with these skirmishes was that very few if any of them lingered past a couple of days, everyone knew the people involved, and there was a beginning and an end to the dispute.

For me the projects were the heaven that the minister spoke of on Sunday morning. There were many occasions when the minister of our Pentecostal Church preached of the joy that we would have in heaven and many of the congregants rejoiced in hearing this. To me I felt that they must have really had it hard where they lived.

"Surely they could not have lived in a project," I thought to myself. Sometimes while eating dinner at the church some of the congregation would openly talk about their trials and tribulations in their neighborhoods. From my perspective I thought that most of their problems could have indeed been resolved if they lived in my version of heaven…"the Forest Projects."

In some respects my connection with the projects conjures memories of a very complicated love affair. Each day there brought tremendous feelings of bliss. You had to feel special living in one of the first projects built in the Bronx. Not everyone realized the importance of this fact. Our project became the pace setter, the lab rat for what other projects would be or some cases, not be.

Little did we know but everything that took place in the "Forest Projects was being scrutinized. They, the authorities, were watching in order to make it better for future projects. They took notice of the civility of the inhabitants toward one another. They wanted to know why we were so civil to one another in some cases, while in other cases we acted like we never knew each other. Secondly they wondered how it was that Blacks and Hispanic people could co-exist in the area without chaos. This may have been a concern because some didn't believe that this was possible. And of course since we lived in such close proximity to one another, eight families on each floor, more questions were raised than were answered.

Somewhere I once heard Lou Rawls say in a song, "your good thing is about to come to an end." In the late 60's my love affair with the project came to a swift end. We were forced out of the projects. All of the details were never quite explained to me being that this was considered "grown folks business." But, from what I gather it had something to do with my brother Sherman, the gangster. Sherman loved the night life and everything that went along with it. Unfortunately for Sherman he got caught up in a situation with some of the fellows that he hung out with. And from what I was told the Ash family was asked to move. For me this was the first major tragedy I remember that we had as a family. For me I was about to lose everything that I held dear. This was catastrophic.

Looking back I considered some of my own reasons for the success of my version of heaven. "Heaven" existed for several major reasons; the maintaining of a consistent veteran security force. The security guards that we had were very skilled in dealing with the inhabitants. They looked like us and identified with us. They gave the appearance that they took several courses in sociology dealing with the family and project dwellers. Armed with simply a nightstick and handcuffs both of which they knew how to use. Among the many security personnel that we had; one in particular stands out. His name was Officer Bagby.

Officer Bagby developed a reputation as a no nonsense type person. In addition to being someone who you avoided, he always seemed to know what was going on. With every situation that Officer Bagby prevented or stopped, his reputation grew. As young folks living in projects, we knew that we had to work hard to conceal things from Officer Bagby. This guy seemed to know a little bit about everything. During one particular incident Bagby was chasing this guy and we were all watching hoping he would get away. Officer Bagby realizing he couldn't catch this guy decided to do something a little different. He suddenly stopped, took out his nightstick and proceeded to hurl it like a boomerang. The stick ended up going between the legs of the young man causing him to stumble and fall. That one skillful act caused us to believe that there was nothing that Bagboy couldn't do. Thus the phrase..."Don't mess with Bagby!"

Another person who formed an indelible impression on me was a guy named Victor. Victor's reputation was based on his ability to run fast. During those days you were not required to have multiple abilities to gain a reputation. Whenever we played our version of tag everyone wanted Victor on their side because he could run so fast. On one particular occasion Victor's skills were really put to the test. It seems that Victor had joined a very well known gang but decided he wanted to quit. Upon realizing that he wanted to quit they informed him that he would have to be subjected to a beat down. At that point Victor pretty much said I'll take the beating if you can catch me. At that point the chase began.

The pursuit of Victor took on the appearance of a Community wide event. There were those of us who believed that none of these guys could catch him. While others believed that because of their determination that they would eventually overtake him. We watched and began to take bets. During the chase we learned a lot about Victor that we didn't know. For instance, not only was he a great sprinter, but he also seemed to possess the endurance of the long distance runner. After awhile it appeared as if Victor was merely playing with them. One by one they began to drop off from exhaustion. Finally the last one ended his pursuit with some threatening gestures and idle threats. Having survived this incident, Victor's name approached legendary status.

Although much was well within the confines of the projects we were not without some tragedies. One such tragedy involved Teddy, the younger brother of one of my brother's friends. The newspapers said he fell to his death from a building. In our community it had been surmised that this young guy had been in a contest of "double dare." This was a game played in many communities at different involvement levels. Apparently Teddy had been dared by someone to leap from one building to another. These were five story buildings where you ascend to the roof and attempt to jump from one building to the other. Much to the regret of one's family, the person attempting this feat only got one chance to get it right. Unfortunately for Teddy he didn't make it.

Early Manhood Training
Physical

My earliest recollection of manhood training came by way of my brother James. From James I feel I learned two things. To begin with I learned how to be smooth. James was the smoothest person that I had known. Among other things James was not known to fight, he was a lover. Living in the projects it seemed like everyone fought. Folks in the neighborhood would fight for what was theirs and also fight for what they wanted to be theirs. This attitude was constant in the hood.

Although James was smooth, he still managed to maintain a viable reputation in the projects. This was realized constantly as he showed no fear while walking through the projects pretty much any time at night. Being out in the projects by yourself late at night earned a male many quality points for courage. This was how James presented himself.

The second thing that I learned from my brother was how to be hard. By this I mean physically hard. James taught me how to take a punch. This was learned through a neighborhood "game" practiced throughout the projects. The "game" was called "chest to chest." This game required you to go one on one with another male. In my case the other male was my brother James. On one particular occasion my brother informed me that he thought I looked like I was getting big and ready to go "chest to chest." Hearing this I was pumped up to go. In this activity we would prepare for close combat in our narrow hallway. Incidentally my mother hated this activity.

The "game" begins with both of us standing toe to toe in our narrow hallway with our arms folded trying to protect our chest. You were only allowed to throw body punches. The game would continue until one of us would decide that he had enough. In other words one of us had sustained enough hard punches and was literally brought to tears. As I got older I got better at this activity, but I was never as good as James.

Although I was never able to beat James at this "game," I did learn a most valuable lesson. I learned that a man should not display outward emotion about internal pain. James never let on whether or not he was hurt. But I never really possessed his level skill. He hit harder and was always a lot quicker than me. All things being equal I was indeed thankful for this lesson in manhood.

It is my belief that my brother, James enjoyed creating a false challenge. In other words he knew that I was not ready to go "toe to toe" with him. Realizing the inner need of a young brother like myself to "prove myself worthy" he would encourage me. "You look like you were working out." "You look like you're getting stronger." "You look like you're ready to go 'toe to toe?'" What young brother, like myself, anxious to become a man would refuse this challenge? "That's right," I would say. Having recently viewed my biceps and triceps in the mirror, I believed that I was ready. "The real question James is, are you ready?" After this last statement from me it was on. Almost immediately we relocated to the narrow hallway.

This physical aspect of manhood I still feel is necessary for most young men. Upon arriving at the hallway we immediately began to cover up. In conjunction with this challenge you had to engage in conversation or "talk trash." This was that rare and often misused ability to describe to someone else what you're about to do to them. "Don't be afraid I won't hurt you too bad." With that comment, I retorted "that's nothing compared to what you will feel."

The first punch was typically just a teaser. We both laughed after exchanging a few initial blows. I am not sure when it happened, but I still remember the impact. It was a blow to the rib cage. I was stunned, much like a fighter just before he gets ready to fall. No matter how much I tried to pretend…I was hurt. The pain was so encompassing that I could no longer verbally retaliate. For some strange reason I found myself constantly saying "okay, okay, okay". The next sign that I remember which alerted me to the fact that I was hurt was I started to tear up. This was an unexpected lesson. **When a man starts to tear up in a physical confrontation…he's in trouble.**

Fortunately for me my mother showed up …just in time. "Stop it; you know I don't like it when you do that James." Although my mother seemingly resented this physical confrontation between two brothers I think she understood it. She had to understand it. If not, why did she show up … just in time?

Early Manhood Training
(Philosophical)

During my early teen years I often sought out any and all types of employment. Fortunately for me my Aunt Frances, who owned a corner store (convenience store), afforded me that opportunity. It was quite common for me to work long and numerous hours per week. For this loyalty I was rewarded more than sufficiently for a young teen. Such rewards included my being allowed limitless hours as a part timer (above the part time limits). Among my many tasks I was asked to walk several blocks to purchase the next day's newspapers for sale at their store.

On one such occasion I traveled the rather lengthy walk up Prospect Avenue to pick up those newspapers. On this particular evening as I made this most fretful walk I encountered some young men, members of a South Bronx social organization (gang) known as the **Diablo Saints.** These young men informed me that they wanted the money that I was carrying to purchase the newspapers. After quickly assessing the futility of my situation I gave up the money. There were at least three of them, I was out of my neighborhood, and I didn't believe that I could out run them. In other words I didn't have a chance of a win. With no money in my pocket a tale of being high jacked by this group I headed home.

Upon arriving home I immediately reported to my brothers James and Sherman. James what had happened. James deferred to Sherman to handle it. Both of my brothers had a very distinct way of dealing with such problems. Sherman asked a number of questions. For a moment I thought I was at the police station being questioned. At the end of the questioning he told me to come with him. To my surprise we marched right back down to the location, 167th street and Prospect Avenue. Yes, it's been over 40 years, but I still remember that most ominous evening. From my perspective I was expecting Sherman to unleash a degree of havoc seldom seen in this part of the Bronx on these guys for them taking my money.

When we reached 167th Street I was excited with the feeling of retaliation. Sherman asked me to point them out. To my amazement they were still standing on the same corner. After identifying them Sherman said for me to wait across the street for him. I didn't mind I figured I could watch my brother from across the street...from a safe distance. To my surprise my brother shook hands with all three of them. Afterwards they talked for about fifteen minutes and he returned back to my location. At that point he informed me that it was done and we headed home. Along the way I couldn't help but wonder, what did I actually bear witness to? Was he afraid of them? Was it to many of them? Did he plan to go back later with reinforcements? With all of these questions on my mind I decided to ask. "Sherman, what happened back there?

For me the response that my brother gave about the meeting proved to be a most valuable lesson of life. He said that he told them that he was my brother and asked them to explain what happened. They said that I offered minimal resistance to their intimidating words so they took my money. Everyone agreed that I had indeed disturbed the equilibrium of the universe by complying without resistance. In other words since I chose not to fight I got what I deserved...empty pockets. Finally, my brother said you will be safe going through this neighborhood now that they know you're my brother.

On that day there were multiple lessons to be learned from this one event. First and foremost prayer alone will not save you. I had prayed that they would not take my money, but they did. I needed to have been an active participant in determining that I wanted to keep my money. In addition I allowed pride to hamper me from surviving with my money. I had seen the young men standing on the corner and all of my instincts pointed to them being trouble, but I did not heed my inner alarm system. And finally, by watching my brother I came to understand that even in the rough and rugged urban centers young men are familiar with the fine art of negotiations.

A Time for Never Again

The arrival of summer in the projects came each year with great anticipation. It was a time for school to close, the anointing of the warm weather to the planet, and in general a time for fun and unfortunately a great deal of mischief. As youngsters at that time we repeatedly sought out different or unusual things to do. One such thing was the acquiring of fireworks. Being in possession of fireworks offered a great challenge to most of the young men in the projects. On the one hand, it was partially illegal, while on the other hand it offered a degree of danger.

Almost every one of the guys in the neighborhood had possession of some type of fireworks. For most this consisted of firecrackers, cherry bombs and roman candles. While these were satisfactory for most still others sought to find something a little different. Most of the people I knew were content to only dabble with the above mentioned types. Although the rest were fascinating as far as most of us were concerned they were a little too dangerous for us to handle. We left that up to the older boys to play with.

Of all the events that took place during the many summers that I spent living in the projects was the summer when I learned the term "never again." It was during that particular summer that I became a victim of foolishness. I literally got caught up in doing things out of my nature. It was for a brief period of time that I thought that I could do all of the things that the other boys in the projects did. So this was one time when I thought I should live vicariously. I became a risk taker. I began to play with firecrackers. I became convinced that I was fearless. Believing in this fantasy would later cost me dearly.

I don't remember where I obtained the firecrackers from, but I acquired them. I would light them up and toss them up in the air just like all of the other boys. After doing that for awhile I found that I began to crave more excitement. I suppose this is what a person does when he is outside of his comfort zone. I began to seek more thrills. Just tossing them in the air seemed too mundane. So I began to throw them at some of the other guys. First it was in the crowd and then I began to get selective. I threw them at one of my friends. But just as quickly that excitement was gone.

I don't know why but for some reason I came up with a brilliant idea of lighting a firecracker and sticking it in someone's pocket. The more I thought about it the more I was drawn to do it. So with the motivation being derived from my inner mind I set the plan in motion. I took out some firecrackers and got real close to the crowd. Meanwhile I had already lined someone up to be the recipient of this most immediate thrill. The person I chose was my next door neighbor, Bill. After lighting the firecracker I very quickly jammed it into his pocket and waited for the explosion. When it exploded he immediately started screaming with a loud screeching scream. Everyone else started laughing and acknowledging that this was the funniest thing that they had ever seen.

Never did I realize that one event would play such a major part in my life for many years to come. As Bill screamed he took off running to his house apparently in a great deal of pain. Just as quickly, I did likewise, heading to my house I found great satisfaction in my accomplishment. After all my deed was a crowd pleaser. Everyone seemed to enjoy the act that I had committed. It was for that brief period of time I felt like a celebrity. But as it turned out my joyous moment was short lived.

It was within that next half of an hour that Bill's mother knocked on our door and asked my brother if my parents were home. My brother not knowing what had taken place called my mother to the door. It was the conversation between these two mothers that made me think that my life was over. After Bill's mother revealed to my mother the horror of what had happened to her son my mother began a series of apologies on behalf of our family. After listening to Bill's mother describe the incident it sounded much worse than I had remembered.

Shortly after Bill's mother left our house my mother called me into her room. To this day I think it was perhaps the worst verbal beating that I ever had. While I listened to my mother chastise me I couldn't erase the image of my father from my mind. With my father in mind I immediately evolved into a prayerful disposition. It was my hope that I could either pray this situation away or pray for forgiveness. For me the most significant part of the evening was my promise. I promised that if I survived, what I knew was coming, a marathon beating; I would never touch another firecracker.

"God, Lord, if I survive the massive beating that is coming at the end of the week on Saturday morning...I will never ever touch another firecracker."

And in forty years I have stood by that promise.

Chapter Three

A Thought

It seemingly lasted for what I believed to be an instant,

But surely it was much longer.

It came, captured my imagination, engulfed my essence,

and then it was gone.

It usurped my creativity, darkened my vision, then it dissipated.

It returns each evening, only to escape with the morning light.

It sometimes invites itself at the most inopportune moment.

It comes and goes at its own bequest.

It has left, but it will reappear.

It can't be denied.

*Then again who really wants to deny…**a thought**?*

Fear of the Unknown

Living in the South Bronx you can become accustomed to many things. For the most part what others may view as unusual you pretty much accept as routine. Although all of this sounds good and may even play well on occasions, but there are those exceptions. One such exception occurred during a summer while I was in high school. It was an evening when perhaps for the first time pure fear permeated the very essence of my being.

Throughout the years that I worked at my Aunt and Uncle's corner store I generally walked home by myself. Sometimes it would be as late as twelve midnight. Having learned the various strategies for survival on the streets of the South Bronx there was never a real concern on my part for my safety. My brothers had taught me how to "walk that way." This particular "walk" let everybody on the street know that you were very self-assured and didn't take any mess.

Therefore no one bothered you while you traveled the streets late at night. Also I was prepped in how to talk to people on the street that you didn't know. Never use complete sentences. You want to give the impression that you really don't have the time to engage in frivolous conversation. Your responses would always be, "Nuh, can't help you, or unh unh." All of which let it be known that I was not interested in their problems.

Having access to all of these tools and skills usually was enough to provide me with that feeling of ultimate comfort. All of this was good until one night when all of these seemed to fail me at the same time.

I had done everything pretty much the same way as always, started my six to eight block trek when it happened. Half way home I was suddenly gripped with an incredible amount of fear. My heart started pumping increasingly faster, thoughts began racing through my mind, and finally a desire to run.

As I began to assess what had changed in my immediate situation, I suddenly realized what it was. It seemed like for the past few minutes I couldn't shake the feeling that this car was following me. When I would walk faster, the car would speed up. For a brief moment I was caught up with some of the old scenario from a Twilight Zone T-V show. It was a scene when a person couldn't shake the feeling that someone was following him. But for me this was very real. This car was definitely following me. Once I came to this conclusion I began to try to figure out why this car was following. Could it be someone who planned to rob me? Or maybe it was someone that wished to do me bodily harm? Worse still was it a psychopath? I couldn't think of anything that closely resembled anything good.

By now I had traveled two blocks and the car was still there. It was then that I decided to take some evasive actions. Quickly I devised a plan. I would make my move when I crossed over Intervale Avenue. I chose Intervale because this street intersected my street Minford Place and I was very familiar with this neighborhood. In addition this was a good area to make a move because there were several alleys in this neighborhood.

Just as I reached my first alley way I made a quick move and darted down this alley. At that instance I heard the sound of a car brakes come to a screeching halt and a door shut. Fortunately for me I had went from a strut to a gallop and rapidly picked up even more speed.

Once I reached my top speed I took great comfort in remembering some old stereotypes about achievements of black people that were scared. One stereotype in particular stood out in my mind. It was a belief that it was very difficult to catch a scared black man. While embracing this piece of historical folklore I'm pretty sure I broke many records for how long it took a person to reach their top speed. Yes I was scared, but I was moving faster than I ever had before.

As I arrived at my destination, my house, I did as many a scared black man had done before me. I began to applaud myself for evading my capture by those who pursued me. And along with these statements I went "ghetto biblical." This term can best be described as altering and distorting biblical parables to suit your individual situation. I am quite sure that everyone uses these phrases like, "blessed is a black man that experiences fear for he will never be caught."

Walk This Way

In its most natural form it seems so simple not a difficult concept to grasp. This was a concept that all of us as humans at one time or another had learned how to do. Some of us can even lay claim to having mastered it. But how many of us realize that there is so much more to walking. There is a lot to learning to walk…to walk this way.

As infants we so often are directed that walking is a part of the maturation process. Before a child learns to walk he must first crawl. He must learn to hold on to something or someone. And if he learns these things he is viewed as functioning within the appropriate norms. However in our household walking involved so much more. It became a way of life. All of the Ash family walked. We pretty much adopted this as a cultural norm.

In the mind of Monroe, the patriarch, the only reason for not walking was if a body of water separated him from his point of destination. My father would walk almost anywhere. In his mind I don't think that there was anywhere that he would not have walked to and from. Being a connoisseur of walking my father developed his own truly unique style... of making it work for him.

Somewhere in his mind my father felt that the shortest distance between two places was achieved by how you walked. He literally became a big stepper. My father took some of the widest steps that you could imagine. In doing this he felt that you had to keep up with him. The thought that his children couldn't keep up with him was unthinkable. Unfortunately for my brothers and me we spent the better part of our youth trying to physically keep up with our father.

This most unusual trait ended up having a truly long-lasting effect on my lifestyle. Throughout my high school years I pretty much walked everywhere. At one point in my life I came to believe that catching buses was what other people did...not men in the Ash family. As a walker I came to believe that I was protected, endowed, chosen, and knew no fear. So serious was this walking contagion that I never worried when I couldn't get a bus or train. During one of NYC's transit strikes I was directed by my father to walk to school. The reality was that this was no small feat. My high school was located in the West Bronx on Fordham Road. In other words it was over 25 city blocks away. On the first day I decided to give it a try...after all it was just walking.

After my extremely late arrival at home my father decided to rethink this strategy. I suspect that he realized that it was a bit much to expect me to use over two hours to go to and from school. I suspect there were two things taking place here. At first that I honored my parents wishes in walking to school. As members of the Ash family we knew our place. The second thing that I bore witness to that first day of the strike was that education was important strike or no strike. I very readily accepted my father's decision to stay home for the remainder of the strike. But from this situation I truly learned to ...walk this way or should I say walk his way.

The Garment District

Somewhere during the course of time I learned to truly appreciate the coming of the summer months. For me the summer represented opportunity. In and of itself there was a chance for a young brother to hone his working skills by seeking out some type of employment. I am still not quite sure why each summer I sought out a different type of employment, but it just seemed to work out that way.

On this one particular summer I managed to secure a job in New York's garment district. This was an area known to be fast paced, full of challenges, and engulfed in the unexpected. Having worked at many other different places I certainly felt that I was up to the challenge. The pace of the job was dictated by the amount of time we were allotted to pick up goods from the warehouse and deliver them to the various shops. Each shop or business that we delivered to had a freight elevator that we used to make this happen. The challenge of the job consisted of how fast you could get these items delivered. In addition management always required you to give an account of your time. It was my understanding that they had already predetermined how long it took for you to deliver the items in your possession. As a worker I quickly came to realize that this business consisted a great deal of mistrust. These guys didn't trust anyone. But it was the third component that bothered me the most… expecting the unexpected. Unfortunately it took a few days to realize what this unexpected was.

It was on this one particular day we were delivering about 100 full length Persian lamb coats. Although they're not really that much a demand for them now, they were much in demand when I worked in the garment district. Myself and two other delivery guys were just getting off the freight elevator when we were confronted by three other African American males. These three guys were very bold. They informed us that they wanted the coats that we were trying to deliver. Our lead guy, who always carried a two foot chain, didn't say anything. At that point the leader of these guys said, "You thinking about doing something with that chain?"

Not being the leader of the delivery group, myself along with the other worker waited for some directions from our leader. For some reason the time between when he spoke and when he stopped twirling the chain seemed incredibly long. While we awaited the decision from our leader the both of us were sweating profusely. I think we kind of knew that if our leader decided to fight we all would have to fight. Besides we had pretty good odds. There were three of them and there were three of us. In essence we were ready.

Fortunately for us the next move was made by the other team. "You guys going to fight for the white man's coats?" I had to smile at this statement. This was a very common ploy utilized during the Black Power days (1960's -1970's) for a brother to challenge your level of blackness. Even though we knew what he was doing we were inclined to agree with him. "This white man don't care about you." From that point they knew they had our attention.

The conversation with our prospective robbers suddenly took on a philosophical approach. "You brothers realize that we are all in the same boat? It's us against them."

With each passing moment our fearless leader appeared to be more in agreement with them than ever. We got the message because he stopped twirling the chain. At that point I knew it was all over. It was then that we went from being victims to becoming prospective accomplices. A feeling that made me feel very uneasy.

So comfortable was this discussion now that it seemed like we were just a group of old buddies having a reunion. Before long I began to feel that we had become co-conspirators with our new found associates. For an instant it looked like we had sold our souls to the devil. At one point they even offered to split the booty with us. "Since you brothers have been so nice about this we would like to split some of the profits with you all."

At that point I knew that someone must have lost their mind. It was bad enough that we were relinquishing someone else's property to these thieves. I didn't care how congenial the conversation had become we were not like them. Even if we gave them the coats we had yet to stoop to their level. We were simply victims who chose to submit because the political climate of the time made it comfortable to delve into that level of complacency.

After we parted our ways, us only with the memories of the event and them with a rack of new Persian lamb coats, we decided to concoct a conciliatory story for our manager. Our fearless leader being a little older and perhaps a little wiser said we had to present a believable story. It was decided that he would tell it.

Myself and the other worker had no problem being silent and allowed him to do the presenting. We quickly learned that he was a great story teller. If I had not been a witness to the robbery I would have very easily believed everything that he said... especially the part about the gun, and that they threatened to shoot us. This part even astonished our manager. "Are you guys alright?" He asked, with a perplexed look.

Looking back there were numerous life lessons to be learned from this very dangerous endeavor. First and foremost don't risk bodily harm for someone else's material things. Although the coats had great value to the company we were sure that the company had insurance on them. Secondly, be sure to know the commitment level toward fighting from your other workers. I was pretty sure that our leader would throw down if he needed to, but I had my concerns about my other worker. So it might not have been 3 vs. 3. It could have been that there would've been three against our two. And finally not having any preconceived ideas on how to handle this encounter let someone else make the decision. My most learned brothers; Sherman and James had not prepared me for this. For me this kind of prep would come later from another…an older mentor.

Too Much Mouth

There was a time when I would dread coming home for the summer. Although it was good to come home to see friends and family there were some other troublesome issues. One of these issues involved dealing with the local corner boys and their constant attempts to engage you in some form of illegal activity. One of my most notable nemeses was Brother Larry.

To understand Brother Larry you had to first understand his background. Larry was a country brother. He had not been long from coming up from one of the southern states maybe South Carolina. Upon arriving in the Bronx he quickly realized what it took to survive. For a "country boy" it was somewhat unusual to find that he had a lot of mouth. In other words he talked too much. It was pretty common for Larry's mouth to get him into something that his fists could not back up. He was a talker not a fighter.

In some respects Brother Larry could be described as being inept in the area of fisticuffs. On one particular occasion he chose to put on a public display of his fighting ability. During this most fateful day he confronted an older brother about something stupid. A very silly argument slowly turned into to something serious. Each one of the brothers began to get loud and very confrontational. Quickly a crowd began to gather on the block. And then everyone began to add their opinion to the ongoing argument.

"You're right Larry, he don't know what he's talking about." With each supporting statement Larry's confidence began to grow in his belief that he was right. As Larry's confidence began to grow he began to challenge the older brother's manhood. Larry started his trash talking. As the argument continued in the torrid heat of a summer day in the Bronx both brothers reached the point of no return. The argument could no longer be resolved with words alone. But for some reason the argument no longer mattered. The older brother felt a challenge to both his manhood and his integrity.

Almost as quickly as the argument started it evolved into the next stage. Just like that the fight was on. Larry threw up his hands and envisioned himself to be the second coming of Muhammad Ali. He swung on the older brother. Not to be denied, the older brother retaliated with a swing of his own. As you can imagine neither one of them had the skills to connect on a first punch. As the crowd began to grow along with their enthusiasm the combatants found new sources of energy. Larry began to dance and shuffle much like the legendary heavyweight champion Muhammad Ali.

"You're old, slow, and can't punch." Along with these statements he would throw three or four jabs in succession while steadily laughing and making light of the situation. The older brother's only response was "Yeah, keep talking young blood." As he withstood taunts the older brother continued his pursuit with increased enthusiasm. "That's right keep coming I'm going to wear that ass out." The more Larry talked the more he appeared to be trying to convince himself that victory was within his grasp, but it wasn't. Unbeknownst to Larry his "trash talking" was taking a toll on his oxygen supply. In other words he was beginning to get tired.

In his mind brother Larry believed that he was endowed with the skills of Muhammad Ali, but the longer he danced the reality didn't seem to support his belief. As the summer sun continued to bare down on both of these black men it was uncertain as to who would be victorious. Although Larry felt that a win was within his reach the crowd didn't really believe it was his to win. It seemed like the longer the battle went on the more winded Larry became. After awhile he could barely talk.

"Youuuuuuuu keep on coming old man." Surprisingly the old man said nothing but simply continued his pursuit. I don't know if it was experience or good old common sense, but the older brother knew that by conserving his breathing he could secure a win.

Within minutes after Larry began stuttering he suddenly threw his hands down and stated, "Old man I ain't got all day to fool with you."

Unfortunately for Larry the crowd didn't seem to be satisfied. They started chanting "Larry, Larry, Larry." Although Larry may have thought that these chants were an indication of approvable for most of us it was simply to make mockery of him losing the fight.

It almost seemed as quickly as the confrontation had begun, that's just how quickly it ended. It appeared that Larry was more in love with the accolades from the crowd than in continuing to pursue the old man. Furthermore I think the fight had reached a point where the verbal support of the crowd was no longer enough to sustain Larry in his attempt to overcome this aging opponent. And then of course there was the reality of all of the energy that Larry had extended in his continuous conversation while he tried to wear this old man down. Plainly said, Larry was simply tired. Fortunately he had saved enough energy so that he could run and get away.

Chapter Four
The Brother's Brother

It's a wonder that the stars don't celebrate the birth of male children; it's astounding that the earth doesn't tilt the other way for every male that enters this world. Perhaps even more disappointing the lack of acknowledgement for the African American male child that survives the birth process.

Statistically we as African American men are expected to achieve very little. There is a rather extensive list of what we don't do, won't do, and can't be depended on to do. The list of negatives sometimes seems almost endless.

In some communities we are pretty much written off from the very beginning. There always seem to be something or someone waiting to short circuit the true potential of the…Black man.

As he strives to achieve through his work experience in America he is quickly engulfed in the turbulent tributaries that await his arrival. For the brother it typically results in a speedy trip to the valley of disappointment.

Should he overcome this obstacle there are pitfalls of the Black man who decides to have a family? What made him think that he could succeed in this venture where so many other Black men have failed and succumbed to the stress of this task? Think not? Just read the newspaper.

What manner of Black man would have the audacity for hope? What manner of Black man would believe that he could beat the odds? What manner of Black man could endure these things and still stand upright and be viewed as a man? According to some your success may only be measured by your attainment of certain positions in life. Or how many salute you on a daily basis.

Perhaps we should consider the strength of a man when he raises a family, more specifically African American males, is loved by his family, respected by other men and recognizes the role that the creator has played in him reaching this milestone of being half a century old. Congratulations Black man on a tremendous accomplishment.

Brotherly Inspiration

There is certainly something to be said for being the youngest in the family. At one time I felt it was more like a curse than a blessing. Being the youngest frequently denied you access to having an identity of your own. You were viewed as someone else's brother, called young Ash, or a sundry of other less than memorable names. None of these names did anything for your self-esteem. On the other hand it could also serve to be a blessing. You were constantly being "schooled" by your older brothers. They seemed to take great pride in telling you about how life worked.

My brother James the master of mind games always seemed to enjoy "schooling" his youngest brother, me. He thought nothing of manipulating you to do something and making you feel good about it. On one occasion he discovered that I was trying out for one of the sports teams.

"I noticed that you have been working out lately, you think you're getting faster? Don't even answer that, I know that you are." That having been said he suggested I run to the store and see if I could get back before the program that we were watching ended.

I was immediately drawn right into this false bravado. "Sure I can." And just like that I was off to the store to pick up some things that he wanted along with some other household items. I was anxious to please. Upon my return he acknowledged the great deal of speed that I must now possess to have gotten back so quickly.

While James may have been a master at manipulating, it was Sherman who truly understood human nature. And it wasn't until many years later that I came to appreciate his possibly innate abilities. It was Sherman who informed me that each one of his friends possessed truly unique talents that he was able to utilize in different situations. Some of his friends were great talkers. They could talk themselves into pretty much anything or out of just about everything. And others were very skillful in games of chance (gambling). These guys knew just how to separate you from your money. Typically they used cards to achieve this goal. And yes they had to be good or they might not eat that night. And then there were the fighters. Usually this was the smallest group. These loyalists, dedicated to the fine art of fisticuffs, you could always count on if you needed someone to fight along your side. And there were times when a young African American male would need to know who he could count on.

The combination of my two brothers, James and Sherman proved to indeed be a most formidable duo of mentors for me. Through them I learned that I could either walk alone or travel with a group. They taught me that if I "walked right" I could always walk along without feeling alone. This technique has certainly served me well over the years as I have had to traverse a variety of neighborhoods.

Then again if I preferred I could travel with a group. During my college days I had the opportunity to experience this aspect of hanging with a group. And it was that time when I remembered the lessons that Sherman taught about understanding the various personalities in your group. It was really nice to realize that everyone in a group that talked about fighting I shouldn't really count on. After all some of them may have been only masquerading as fighters and were perhaps better at something else.

During one very pivotal point in my life Sherman revealed something unbelievable to me. He informed me that all of his "boys" could not fight. This to me was shocking. I found it hard to envision that some of these guys that he hung out with couldn't fight. Upon learning this I had to ask, "Why do you hang out with them?" At that point he chose to enlighten me on another facet of life.

"Every one of my friends serves a purpose." Some of them are fighters, others lovers, gamblers, and finally you have some wannabes. Seeing that I didn't get it he went on a little further. You need some fighters because when you leave the safety of the projects you need to know who you can count on … If you get into something. As for lovers they come in handy because they always know how to attract women … and that never hurts. And then there are the gamblers who can always make sure that we can get money when we are broke. Gamblers are generally more inclined to be risk takers. They know how to win. And lastly there are the wannabes. Seldom does anyone else think much of this group. Wannabes are usually lowlifes. They will generally do just about anything to belong…legal or illegal.

When he finished explaining this bit of reality I had to ask one more question. How do you know who is who? He replied over time you will learn how to do these assessments. But he left me with this warning. "Be careful not to get the classifications confused. Don't mistake the lover for a fighter. The lover will most certainly run when it's time to fight."

The Art of Attraction

The fine art of attraction is at best a very delicate and difficult process. There is many a young man who has attempted to claim to be an authority in this particular area. "I got plenty women", "I can get anyone of them that I want", or "I could have been a pimp if I wanted to with all of the game that I got." These statements and many more I have heard over the years from both my associates and friends. But for me none of them came close to the level that my brother James maintained. Although I know he didn't go to school to study this complicated field of study I was always sure that he must have earned a Ph.D.

from the streets. No matter how you looked at it my brother was a doctor of love psychology.

Although I always viewed him this way, he never seemed to show any signs of being vain. He always seemed more than willing to show both me and Sherman his very high skill level in this particular Art. In each lesson we both acquired techniques that could best be described as priceless. On this one particular occasion he explained that you had to be somewhat suave and debonair in order to attract the right type of women. You could never give the appearance of being a hoodlum or a lowlife. Most of the "nice" women found nothing attractive about these types. Guys who were suave never really talked too much or too loud. They were cool.

In addition this particular group always dressed a certain way. Never would they allow themselves to be caught wearing anything loud and outlandish. Their clothes didn't have to be expensive, but they couldn't be cheap either. The pants were generally done in earth tones, shoes black or brown, and shirts typically were done in a light blue or even yellow; if your skin tone could tolerate it. James generally stayed away from yellow. For some reason it didn't really work with dark skinned brothers. And my brother was as dark as me.

On still another occasion James told us that women looked at the type of women that you attract. "If there are no attractive women in your stable of women you can't expect to attract any." That seemed pretty clear, but still a little difficult to grasp. This statement immediately generated some questions in my mind. How do you know that women that you deal with are attractive or not? Isn't it true that beauty is in the eye of the beholder? At least that's what I always heard.

With this question James began to laugh. "Stan, that's incredibly easy to answer.

You've been away at college for one whole year now, right? That's true, and? How many women have sent you a picture of themselves? A lot, right?"

"Yeah, get to the point."

When your male classmates come to your room and see the pictures, what do they say? Do they give sounds of approval? If they do that's good. That having been said, what do your female classmates say when they see the pictures? You see in this case it's also important as to what the women say. Remember women like to know that other women are attracted to you too.

It was my intention to absorb and if possible to emulate this master tactician, but apparently that was not my Brother Sherman's plan. Although we both heard the message and literally inhaled every word Sherman didn't have the same reaction. In observing the type of women that Sherman had in his flock there was a decided difference from the women in James' circle. James' women were more refined and apparently had come from excellent stock. While Sherman's women were always a little rough at the edges. Generally James burnt them off or extricated them from his files a lot faster than Sherman. In addition I don't recall that James ever had any type of altercation with his women. This was not the style of a love doctor. On the other hand I noticed that it was not uncommon for Sherman's "girlfriend" to show her love by breaking his glasses. After the incident with Sherman and his girlfriend, I knew that by following James I would fare a lot better. I didn't think that I could tolerate Sherman's kind of relationships.

One of the most remarkable aspects of all of this teaching by James was that it was free and from someone that I trusted...my brother. I couldn't help but wonder and feel sympathy for other males who didn't have access to an older brother with so much knowledge. How can it be possible for a young man to avoid all of these numerous pitfalls of the "art of love", if he doesn't have a male Love Doctor in his corner? Can a woman, sister or mother impart all of this knowledge on their son or brother? Thankfully I never had to experience such a situation.

Book of James

For all practical purposes my brother James could certainly be viewed as the Love Doctor. To me James seemed to know all anyone could hope to know about women. So skilled was he with his talent that he never appeared with any women that could not be deemed attractive. In addition he managed to stay on top of the latest dances. He didn't seem to care what culture or ethnic group was doing the dance. You might want to call him a connoisseur of fine women.

It was quite common to find James constantly fine tuning his method of pursuit. A major part of his strategy involved the dance. James would practice constantly the latest style of dances. When questioned he had a most unusual way of simplifying things to its most basic component. Once I questioned him about how he learned to hold a girl when dancing with her. In his most unenviable way he replied that you needed a broom. With that thought in mind he immediately grabbed a broom and proceeded to show me how it was done. He said take your right hand and hold the broom about mid way down with a firm but gentle grip. Then he proceeded in suggesting that you take the left hand and hold the top of the broom. The last part was the most difficult. You had to have the wherewithal to do a 360 degree turn and catch the broom before it fell to the ground.

In addition James maintained a view that he had to constantly replenish his arsenal with increasingly more difficult "moves". To this day I still believe that one of the most endearing experiences was to watch this "master" at work. You see for all of what he showed or previewed at home it was nothing compared to watching the master at work on the dance floor. I don't think that I viewed him as a master because he was my brother, but it was more about how he matched up with the competition on the dance floor. In the African American community it was always about your skill level compared to the others on the dance floor. You didn't have to be the best, but certainly should not be viewed as the worst.

On one most memorable weekend, I had a chance to watch the "master" at work. Oh, this was one of the highlights of living in the projects. This activity did not involve females arguing, male fights, or family feuds. This very simply put was pure unadulterated dancing...dancing until you drop. In some respects it was perhaps a precursor to what later we called break dancing with some subtle differences. Some differences involved your style of dress. You had to be immaculate from head to toe. Your hair typically had to have a process or sometimes called a conk. Shirt was made of silk, if you could afford it. If you didn't have one you borrowed one from someone else. Pants had the best crease that the cleaners could provide. I don't think that there was anything such as a special crease, but we would ask for it anyway. And then there were the shoes. The shoes added the final touch to how you would be viewed by neighborhood locals. Your choices consisted of either lizards or gators. It really didn't matter which one you chose. Finally you were ready to leave the house. Since all of this activity took place in the projects it was a short walk to the neighborhood center, about five minutes.

The arrival at the neighborhood center at first did not seem too special, at least not at first. The magnitude of the event didn't really reveal any real significance until the masters arrived. In today's terms they were seen as rock stars. On these occasions there was a multitude of women there. Much like their male counterparts they too came to this affair in their finest clothing that they could find. These women wanted to have this event on their resume that they were in attendance at least at one of these events. Part of the wonder of these type events was that on any given night one of the old masters could be unceremoniously dethroned and a new master anointed. As for the males that attended these events their reasons were slightly different than the women. For the males they wanted to have the experience of being there. Secondly, they hoped that one of their boys would become acknowledged as one of the new masters. Or, maybe they wished to test their own talents against the best on the dance floor. Everyone jammed into this center and waited for the music to start.

For the most part the music started out with just a little bop. It seemed like everyone there could bop. Subsequently the floor was packed. This went on for a short period of time before the disc jockey began to infuse some Cha cha in the mix. With the infusion of the Cha cha some of the dancers began to maneuver their way off of the dance floor. It appeared that not everyone was comfortable with the energy required to keep up with this Latin flavor of music. After about an hour or two the dance participants went from about fifty couples down to about ten. Throughout these initial stages of bop and Cha cha everyone seems to have found their comfort level in show casing their dance abilities. But this was how the dances always started. They started out with the preliminaries in order to give everyone an opportunity to dance. The last hour would be devoted to the "masters".

In an effort to rid the floor of the rookies, second stringers, or the wannabes, the music changed to a well defined heavy Latin beat. During this time only the Latin classics were played. During this last hour artists such as Jimmy Valentin, Tito Puente and one of the all time favorites Joe Cuba were featured. It was just some-thing special about Joe Cuba during that era. The song that was chosen was Azucar Para Ti. Loosely translated it meant Sugar for You. One of the more fascinating things about the song was the length. It was about 17 minutes long. To be able to dance to this song was truly a work of art, a test of endurance, and to be sure an opportunity to display your mental fortitude.

When "Azucar Para Ti" came on everyone knew that it was the last song of the evening. Almost immediately everyone began to form an impromptu circle around the "masters". On that evening there were five recognizable masters all from different sections of the Bronx. At this point the evening took on the appearance of a professional competition. You could be certain that there would be plenty of cheers and little, if any jeers.

The song "Azucar Para Ti" was a very popular song used at dance competitions during this time. Some of its popularity stems from the length. Along with its length came a very continuous beat. In addition the singer was very popular. Joe Cuba at this time was one of the hottest Latin singers in the New York area. And finally a lot of the competitors had used this song to practice for the event. All in all everyone knew that the final song would be Joe Cuba's Azucar Para Ti.

Although the evening ended with a three way tie, I think everyone was satisfied with the results. In the room that evening there was certainly a great deal of bias. All of the judges had their favorites in the competition. The women in the audience knew who they wanted to win. But in the end it was the wisdom of the neighborhood center directors who realized that if any one person was going to be declared the winner it would not happen in the heat of July. In their infinite wisdom they knew it would be better for everyone to leave the center believing that the talent was so great the judges were unable to decide on one particular winner.

Thin Line Between Love and Hate

Sometimes as children begin to come of age...so too do their parents. Successful parents are at times called upon to make difficult decisions. They are asked to do things which may be viewed as cruel and unusual punishment. Perhaps that is why there never is a long list of candidates wanting to become parents. Add to that there is even a shorter list of men trying to jump in front of each other to become...fathers.

Although Monroe Ash may not have been accused of rushing upfront to become the next father in line he certainly knew what to do once it became his turn. Much of what he did implied he was indeed groomed to serve in that capacity. One of the more arduous tasks of fatherhood for most men is generally the art of making the tough decision. The ability to be able to stand in front of your family, community and sometimes the world and say…I've made my decision.

On one particular occasion, my father had to make a most difficult decision about one of my brothers, Sherman. It was revealed that Sherman had broken several rules in the eyes of my father and for this there was a price to pay. At these times manhood becomes difficult. Among other things Sherman had been staying out later and later each night. It seems that Sherman had reached that awkward position of being eighteen, out of high school, and still living at home. With all of these things going on Sherman had concluded that he was "grown." Unfortunately for Sherman he didn't realize much like many other young men had to learn an unwritten but very credible reality. There can only be one man per household.

As if staying out late wasn't bad enough, Sherman begun to grow more and more brazen with his violations. His final violation that forced my father to make a decision was the taking of someone else's property. Sherman had a need for some money so he stole some of my mother's jewelry. With this act of thievery my father decided that he had had enough. In a very brief family meeting between my father, mother, and Sherman my father informed him that he had to find somewhere else to live. Not being privy to this meeting, my information was arrived at by the clandestine format of...eavesdropping.

Although I knew it was necessary my father's decision left me somewhat befuddled. You see Sherman had been diagnosed with kidney failure and was told he would have to go on dialysis. With this newly diagnosed health condition I was sure that my father would show some degree of leniency and allow Sherman to stay. Later I would learn that in my father's eyes Sherman's stealing was tantamount to committing a felony. My father viewed himself as being the judge, jury, and the one to carry out the sentence. The decision was made. He had to go regardless of his health issues.

In viewing what I viewed as a very intricate process of separation I was learning that manhood should not be taken lightly. Although my mother was upset about my brother's stealing her jewelry she was equally concerned about putting him out. If given a choice I think that she would have forgiven him and allowed him to stay. But I think that Sherman became torn between doing what he wanted to do and being bold enough to challenge the real man of the house…our father.

Throughout the next morning, after Sherman's departure, I did a lot of soul searching. What did all of this mean for me? Where was the Ash family that I once knew? I think that it was in the late hours of the evening that I was able to unravel some of the day's proceedings regarding the exit of still another member of the Ash family. Life was becoming incredibly real. The fantasy of the happy ending was quickly dissipating.

It was my determination that some of the things that I had witnessed was part of a natural evolutionally process. Children growing up and doing some things that their parents disagree with was not that unusual. All children have this potential and some realize this sooner than others, but it happens. Secondly, parents are not always going to agree on things that should be a no brainer. When someone steals there must be a penalty to pay. And finally, manhood/fatherhood is not something that every male should eagerly rush into once you arrive at that station in life there is no turning back or do over. Once a male declares his manhood he will be expected to confront some of the most unusual and bazaar problems he has ever seen.

There was much to be learned from witnessing the clash of a father who truly understood manhood and a son striving to get there. Prior to embarking on this rode of no return Sherman had concluded that he now had his own opinions, could make his own decisions and generally longed for his own domain. All that having been said I think he believed that our mother would save him from the wrath of our father. With most things Sherman was a quick witted gifted thinker, but in this case these abilities did not trump my father's decisive actions.

Chapter Five

Trash Talking

*Few humans on the planet can exchange words like men,
But it gets even deeper when it involves black men.
We are commonly known to complete sentences
before the other brother does,
Or claim to have known what he was thinking before he said it.
Sometimes we are just...**talking trash**.*

*With brothers there are very few if any subjects that we won't challenge,
We seek to be authorities on a wide variety of things, while seldom
Admitting to not being up on a certain subject or issue.
We love to...**talk trash**.*

*We are never bashful when engaging someone in an unfamiliar subject.
If we lack the immediate knowledge on a particular subject,
We know how to fake it.
Should the material become overwhelming we most
Readily resort to...**trash talking**.*

*For brothers we are constantly searching for new venues to
Engage in thought provoking conversation.
Perhaps one of the most unusual occasions available is when
putting out the trash.*

*For men it offers a very relaxed, non-committal, free time arrangement.
During this time and place a brother can do his thing.
In addition he may have added a new definition to
...**trash talking**.*

The Story of David
Value of Family

So often is the value of family taken for granted that there is really no need to discuss this sad and unfortunate statistic. The reality of it all can be somewhat mind boggling if you allow it. The family ties don't always have to be that strong. Sometimes even the weakest strand can be enough to insulate an individual from one of the most tragic situations that society can toss at him.

I am reminded of a most unusual situation that took place many years ago. I often refer to it as a biblical experience. For many years while growing up, I recall hearing about David while in Sunday school. At that time I really did not pay much attention to the whole story of David. Little did I realize that "David" would appear in my life at a very opportune time in my life?

While attending Theodore Roosevelt high school in the Bronx I found that I had very few truly worthwhile values. But, there was one thing that I truly valued while a teenager. I truly valued going to parties. I was determined to attend every party that I could while in high school. On some occasions I would travel with a group. Sometimes we were twelve deep, but for the most part I traveled alone. Besides, not every household would allow a group of twelve males to come to their house uninvited.

On one such occasion I was invited to a party in a neighborhood that I was not quite familiar with. Although for some this might have served as a deterrent, for me it served as stimulus for what a great party it could be. That having been said I went anyway. And I was indeed glad that I did. There were plenty of girls there and very few fellows. Later in life I used this as a lesson to determine when to stay and when to go.

I was having such a good time that I became a little too lax. Here was another lesson to be learned. Every party that I have ever attended had consequences. This one was certainly no different. It was not logical that with all of these females there, that there would not have been more males. Where were all of the males from my school? What about the brothers from the neighborhood?

Somewhere around 11:30 I began to get some answers to these perplexing questions. It seems that the young lady giving the party was upset with the fellows in the neighborhood so she didn't invite any of them. Almost immediately I knew that this was potentially a very bad situation. Being a party person I knew that you had to invite some of the fellows from the "hood." This was a major oversight on her part.

Soon after this everyone in the house heard from the fellows outside who were not invited. There was easily about a half dozen of them proclaiming that they were going to do bodily harm to any of the fellows that they caught leaving the party. The tone of their voices and their choice of words made me realize that I now had a problem. At this particular time there was one "brother", who decided that he didn't care what they said, he was ready to leave and they were not going to take his heart. So he did just that, he left.

When this brother got outside all we heard was a serious verbal exchange of profanity. The tone of which led me to believe that he did not handle all six of these fellows. In other words he took a serious beat down.

After realizing the potential for what could happen I quickly began to go into a defensive mode of thinking. No longer was I concerned about when the next slow jam was going to come on or which young lady I had not danced with. I was trying to save my butt. With this thought in mind I did what any serious brother would do ...quietly pray! I prayed the contemporary prayer of "Why me?" and "How did I get into this situation?" and "How am I going to get out of this one?"

For what it was worth I pretty much had answers for the first two, but it was the third question that concerned me. How was I going to get out of this?

It was at this instance that I suddenly had a revelation. A brother stepped to me and introduced himself as David and then asked a very enlightening question; what are we going to do? Being somewhat inclined, like so many others do when in trouble, to make biblical connections to everything, I knew that my prayer had been answered with the appearance of David. I knew that this certainly must have been divine intervention.

Almost immediately David and I devised a plan "to overcome". We had decided that we would come together for there was strength in numbers. This new found unity indeed proved to be a force to be reckoned with. A decision was made that as soon as the opportunity presented itself we would run downstairs and run. Sometimes there is no shame in running. "A good run still trumps a bad stand."

As the number of people at the party began to dwindle we decided that the two of us, although we didn't come together, would leave together. Fortunately for us there was a brother there from another part of town who declared that he was no punk and that he was leaving the way he came, by himself. At that point, David and I very cautiously observed this brother's departure. When he got downstairs he was immediately confronted by this group. A few words were exchanged then he decided it was time to run. I interpreted his running as a sign from up above for me and David to make our exit. We calmly walked out the door and proceeded to run down the stairs. When we got downstairs, we could hear those most uncomfortable disturbing words that concern every black man..."get that mother _____".

Coming out of the doorway we quickly realized that another blessing was bestowed upon us. They were going in the opposite direction of which we wanted to go. At that point we took off running. It was a long run, about 7 to 8 blocks. I suspect that the combination of fear + adrenalin + prayer = superhuman abilities. We hardly noticed that we traveled such a great distance. By now we were at the train station. David and I shook hands, laughed and he proceeded to catch the train back to

Harlem. I continued on for two more blocks before I reached the safety of home.

On Monday when I saw David at school he took the approach that brothers typically take. He stopped in the hallway on the way to class, gave me a high five, and acted like the event was just a day in the life of living in an urban center. As I moved on to my next class, I learned that there were some lessons to learn from this party. For one, be mindful about attending a party by yourself in another neighborhood. These situations offer the potential for a lot of things going wrong. Secondly, be prepared for the unknown. What if something unexpected comes up? What do you do? And finally pray, but also be prepared to receive the solution. David was the answer to my prayer.

Obtaining Friendship

Many a man has sought to find, secure, and obtain that most lofty goal of making a friend, but few really seem to know the various nuisances involved in this process. Within this realm there appears to be several things that need to be taken into consideration. In order to obtain this title from the male perspective, typically the two of us would have to have experienced something that perhaps is truly unique to the two of us. Generally speaking these things are sometimes dangerous, clandestine, or awe inspiring.

During the 1960's one of my buddies moved to the level of becoming a "friend."

This change in status was the direct result of an experience that he and I shared. On one particular Saturday morning, I called on my buddy, Ralph, to go with me to the Wonder Bread outlet. Going to the Wonder Bread bakery was no small task. To begin with it was outside of the protective confines of the "projects." This alone was a major hurdle for most young men in our project. Add to that it was several blocks away. For two young males to make a move like this was extremely daring and dangerous. It was ventures like this that made me understand why black parents always prayed so much. And then there was the consideration that we had to cross through at least two other neighborhoods… where we didn't know anyone. But much like Kunta Kinte in Roots we didn't always heed the warnings from either our parents or even our elders. We were excited about what seemed like a great adventure.

In order to get to this bakery outlet we had to go past several uncharted areas. On the way there we went past Morris High School the school that my oldest brother and sister attended. This was significant because neither one of us had ever been past this location. As we walked past the high school both of us began to laugh with youthful excitement at our new found bravado; two courageous young men leaving the safety of the Forest Projects. Almost instinctively we began to talk about the story we would tell our classmates on Monday morning about how we were not afraid to leave the projects and go to this bakery... by ourselves. Yes, we were pumped and beeming with the encouragement that we indirectly bestowed upon each other. Two buddies slowly developing into...Friends.

Several blocks later we arrived at the bakery with a feeling of great accomplishment. From what I can recall it seemed like the cashier realized that we were not from that neighborhood and that we were inexperienced shoppers. The look on our faces told a story of young boys out on an excursion… perhaps for the first time.

"Yes may I help you?" the cashier asked. By now we couldn't contain ourselves.

We immediately began to laugh, "We would like some chocolate donuts."

We had no idea how many and no idea what they cost. For a brief moment the cashier began to laugh with us, or at us. We were never really sure which it was, but we didn't care. We ended up leaving the bakery with about four boxes of donuts. Both of us liked the chocolate frosted donuts.

We were so excited by our accomplishment that we completely forgot about all the rules of survival that we were taught by the "old heads" or project elders. We had forgotten that the world is a dangerous place, there is greater safety in numbers, and that there is no place like your home projects. Unfortunately for us it didn't take too long for the reality of where we were to set in. About two blocks past the bakery we saw guys standing in front of a store. We looked at them and they in turn looked at us. At this point we were no longer smiling. Much like an animal in the jungle can sense when the atmosphere has suddenly changed we quickly realized it was now time to prepare for the unexpected. We had trespassed into someone else's territory. Although we sometimes quote scripture when we see trouble on the horizon, "forgive those who trespass against us as we…" but in this case we didn't have time to try to remember the exact words.

As we walked a little further we came to realize that those guys were now following us. One of the lessons that we learned from the elders was "a good run beats a bad stand any day." This philosophy would somehow outlast the suggestions that had come from our friends, "I'll stand and fight rather than run." For most it always seemed that the former was practiced a lot more than the latter. We figured we could always adjust the story to the expectations of what our friends wanted to hear. Somehow we figured our survival rested more with a good run. With this in mind we began to run. At that point we noticed that they began to run too.

After about two blocks we could tell that these guys were really getting angry. Maybe it was because they couldn't catch us or maybe because we were now laughing as we ran. As we neared Morris High School we came to realize that we would have to climb back over this fence. With this thought in mind our smiles began to dissipate. For it was at this juncture that we saw the possibility of getting caught. When we initially came over the fence it was a lot easier. Now we had to do it on the run. This required a different level of skills. We now had to hit the fence with one foot and then kind of catapult ourselves over. As we neared the fence we threw the donuts over first and then proceeded to place one foot in the fence and push ourselves up and over. Upon reaching the other side it was as if all our sins were forgiven and we were given two tickets to heaven.

Once over the fence we were subjected to an incredible amount of profanity and verbal threats. All of the other guys remained on the other side of the fence promising what they would do to us if they ever caught us in their neighborhood again. Biblically speaking we had reached the promise land and evaded our adversaries much like Moses had done to the Egyptians. None of that mattered to my buddy Ralph and me. We were now friends safely approaching the protective confines of the Forest Projects…our promised land. Truly there is no place like home.

The Beginning of the End

All of my brothers were fascinating to me, but James offered a series of unique perspectives on life. For it was he who could make things appear to be not as bad as they seemed. He always looked like he had a plan. At least that was what I thought until he decided to confront our father. I don't think there ever was or ever will be a man who could frighten me like my father, Monroe Ash.

On this one occasion James had either accidently or on purpose broken one of our father's rules. I don't recall which one it was, but James swore he was not afraid of the repercussions. I think that having withstood other beatings from our father, he thought that he could withstand anything that my father could bring his way. This indeed was going to be a show down. Add to the fact that all of this took place on a weekday...not on judgment day.

In an effort to prepare for the onslaught James began to pump himself up. He began to profess his bravado. I think that he thought between his increased adrenalin flowing and by calling up for more testosterone that he would be ready. Unfortunately it proved one of the worst evenings for the Ash family while living in the projects. I am quite sure that our neighbors thought that the Ash family was engaging in an all out war.

Although our father never grew any taller or heavier, his overall demeanor remained consistent. I have never known him to show any fear of any of us. This was a man thing.

Perhaps a man's commandment, 'thou shall not fear thy children'.

Thus when called to my father's room to give an accounting for his misdeeds James had no problem confessing. It was then when my father announced his sentence. Most of my father's punishments involved something physical…a beating. Monroe was never big on punishment involving restricting privileges. In that sense he maintained that a good beating could solve and resolve most if not all of what your problems may have been.

It was at that time when James became even bolder. He began to declare to my father that he was sixteen and that he was too old to get beatings. I don't know why he said that, but I suppose that's when I realized that my other brother (Sherman) and I better get out of the way.

By now my father had taken his belt out to carry out the punishment. And for the first time ever James did not submit to my father's will. At that moment my father summoned my oldest brother, Monroe Jr. to grab James and to hold him. Now James became really hyped and told Junior to let him go. Unfortunately for James my oldest brother Junior had sided with my father and was committed to restrain James.

As for my other brother Sherman and I we just watched in shear disbelief. For us this was the first time anyone in our house had challenged our father. Meanwhile my mother, Frederica, was hysterical. I think that all of us were uncertain as to what was going to happen next. James had broken all of the household laws that we could imagine; those stated and unstated.

The only thing that I kept thinking about was…"honor thy mother and father." Even as bold as Sherman was he never ventured to cross that line and was I certain that he never would...or so I thought. Sherman and I both believed that whatever the outcome of this evening...James was done and perhaps so was the Ash family as we knew it.

In my mind there were a series of harsh lessons learned that evening. For so long as we had been a family ruled by our father, Monroe, the patriarch, the family would remain a viable unit. And for us this had worked with very few deviations. In addition I learned that every young man...and some young women reach the point of no return. Giving in to their attitude, disposition, or simply a yearning to say or do something that they desire; that they venture into a very dark area. James had "gone there." He sought to challenge the master of his domain...our father. Life would never be the same.

It was not until much later in life that I would learn that it was necessary for a man to stand by his principles...right or wrong. Although we may never have agreed on all of what he did and how he did it Monroe's beliefs helped to sustain a family of five children during some very difficult times. Although we, as children, were tempted to do "the wrong thing," we never really strayed too far from the right thing. Thank goodness for Monroe Ash.

Minford Place

If the projects could best be described as Heaven then surely Minford Place could be viewed as something on the other end of the spectrum. Looking back there were few, if anything that I can think of that was favorable about the place. In order to best understand my view of this "place" it would be best that I describe what made me feel this way about this neighborhood.

The street consisted of about three city blocks. Each one of these blocks appeared to be overcrowded with "folks"; a hodgepodge of various ethnic groups; Blacks, Hispanics, some Asians, and others of unknown origin. Along with this mixture of folks came an incredibly lost and downtrodden disposition. These folks were very content with where they were in life. No one seemed to care about themselves or anyone else. On a given day very few people on the block even went to work. In some respects they appeared to be residing in purgatory waiting for the next train to hell. They showed little concern as to whether they lived or died. Perhaps they were dead already.

Economically many of the residents owed their souls to the local corner store. From my perspective most of the residents had an account at the local Hispanic corner store. Almost all of the local children ...and their parents had a "credit" account at that store. Later I was to learn that this merchant allowed the local families to buy groceries on "credit"; in other words until their check came in at the first of the month. Apparently this was a practice that takes place in many urban centers around the country where many of the residents are on fixed income. All of this may have been okay for most, but for me it was terrible. You see the system was not monitored and certainly not legal. That having been said it reeked with corruption. Subsequently, no one should have been surprised to discover that the amount that the residents said they owed did not always jibe with what the store owner said. Unfortunately for the residents it was always resolved in the favor of the store owner. If the residents didn't go along with the store owner's numbers their "credit" account was closed.

Another strange anomaly of Minford Place was that no one controlled the neighborhood. The adults could care less. The children had no direction and the merchants were pretty much satisfied with the status quo. But unfortunately for everyone this could not continue for long. It seems that a local group of drug addicts decided to take advantage and commence to robbing the homes of the locals much to the dismay of the residents. In some respects the residents never understood the adage "you're either part of the problem or you're part of the solution."

The residents from my point of view were part of the former. In contemporary sports lingo they did not meet the energy of the addicts with an equal amount of their own energy.

Fortunately for me I was on my way back to school and had little time to ponder the problems of Minford Place. In my mind I knew that the Ash household would survive. Besides there were other situations that did not destroy the fabric of our family so I felt rather secure boarding the plane to go back to Doane College. Minford Place would continue to be Minford Place…or so I thought. Never did I imagine the turn of events that I would have to confront upon my return.

With the coming of the summer in 1968, I welcomed the opportunity to return to my roots...the Bronx. The Bronx offered comforts that only a true native New Yorker could truly look forward to. After all there was something special about living in an area where every day you had to confront the unexpected, the unanticipated, and the unwanted. This was the New York that I had come to adore. Few, if any outside of my domain, could identify with what may have looked like insanity to many, but it was home for me. This was how I viewed the Bronx; more specifically the South Bronx.

Unfortunately for me being at Doane had an unsuspected impact. Unbeknownst to me I had become devoid of most of the skills of survival that I left New York with. I now found it difficult to anticipate and confront the unsuspected. Although I had never bore witness to this unique phenomenon I had heard of it happening to other brothers from Chicago,

Los Angeles, and even Panama City. According to these others they say that you lose your edge as a result of being in a rural area for an extended period of time. Some even described it as a distortion of your senses. Everything that I once took for granted and had little apprehension about now made me extremely nervous. I was still Black, but exhibited similar reactions to my neighborhood that suburban Whites did.

Although I knew both the Bronx and to some extent Minford Place this time it did not seem the same. I could not sense immediately what had changed, but something was different. It was the summer and the block should have been a lot nosier...but it wasn't.

On the front step of my apartment building was an elderly man who upon my asking was more than willing to tell about the "new Minford Place." Why is it so quiet out here? What happened to the drug addicts that used to roam the street?

"Oh, they don't hang out here any more."

"What happened?"

"The Jolly Rogers!"

After a brief explanation he informed me that a group of teenagers had gotten together and formed a group or gang called the Jolly Rogers and they were attacking any addicts that they found on the block.

"Sometimes they beat them up real bad."

"How do the neighbors feel about these 'Jolly Rogers'?"

"They love them because they chase the addicts off the block."

It wasn't too long before I got a chance to see the "Jolly Rogers" in action. The following evening being a Friday, some of the addicts accidently ventured into the Minford Place neighborhood. Unfortunately they, along with me, got a chance to bear witness to the influence of the Jolly Rogers. In what looked like a scene from a Hollywood production two teenagers were in hot pursuit of a man who was identified as a drug addict. In an effort to put fear in him they repeatedly used a barrage of profanity along with anything they could throw in his direction to let him know what they thought of him. Even as a native New Yorker I found this whole event a bit farfetched. The whole idea of a so called "good guy gang" chasing the bad guys?! For me this was somewhat unimaginable.

The Chosen One

And it came to pass, one of the more enduring phrases that can serve as a great inspiration, "that the last would be first and the first would be last". It only seems natural that someone would be the first...the first to begin the college educational experience. After much thought and consternation I began to embrace this most novel concept...the first, the lab rat, the Guinea Pig or perhaps better still; the Chosen One!!!

Unbeknownst to me being the first brought along with it some interesting perks. One such perk was an extra dose of prayers from the church congregation. At first it didn't seem that significant, but this impression was certainly to change after a few months at Doane. The Doane College experience was quite a lot for an African American male from New York City to endure subsequently the prayers certainly became a most valued ally.

Another benefit that I received from both family and community was that of recognition. It seemed like everyone attached a great deal of pride to this accomplishment. Oddly enough I didn't really get it. From my point of view I had not accomplished anything as of yet. All I did was to get accepted.

I remember thinking, "Suppose I don't make it? Will all of these folks still be happy with my just having been accepted only to return to the neighborhood with no degree?" That thought did manage to dwell on my mind for some time.

Over the years I have come to realize that it is still viewed as a tremendous accomplishment in many African American households. Simply getting to college can earn many brothers many accolades.

In addition to everything else I found that this accomplishment did a lot for filling up my social calendar. In other words the girls loved to be connected to a "college guy". I think that in the Black community most mothers thought that their daughters had found the pot of gold at the end of the rainbow. Even then mothers, and some fathers, were concerned about their daughters connecting with some very viable candidates that showed potential for a long term relationship…otherwise known as husband material. With so many "brothers" adhering to the contemporary jargon of the time such as "I am trying to get myself together" or "I am trying to find myself"; parents had a need to be concerned with the lack of focus of many of young men at this time.

And finally the reception that one received from the "brothers" was unique. For the most part "brothers" didn't know whether to congratulate you or hate you. In keeping with the uncertainty of an appropriate response they generally just said something like, "at least you don't have to go to "the Nam." All of the brothers that I knew were concerned about having to go to Viet Nam. For the most part they felt that said it all.

Perhaps one of the most pivotal parts of this whole College thing hit me a few days after I got accepted. Where was I going to get the money to pay for this…College education! At that time Doane was considered to be one of the best deals out there. The cost of Doane was $1,950.00 per year. It is hard to believe that was all it cost back then. Although it may not seem like a lot, but for a poor African American family living in the South Bronx it was a lot. But being a prayerful family we believed that somehow we would get the money.

The acquisition of the money to begin the higher educational process came from a most unusual source. If poor folks don't believe in nothing else we do believe that the lord will provide. And one night as I sat in my parent's room contemplating how to get this money we got a surprise visit from my eldest brother... Monroe, Jr. To understand Monroe was to realize that he was different. In today's terms he would have been diagnosed as Special Ed. During those days they didn't have "special classes," they had something for "those who didn't quite get it."

In spite of what some may have thought about Monroe he did indeed do things "differently." He seldom, if ever, truly communicated with other members of the household. On most days he kept to himself and didn't bother anyone. But for some unknown reason he heard the call that his family was in need of financial relief. Perhaps it was predestined that there would be an unusual connection between the first and last born. On that particular morning Monroe did step up, step forward and did something memorable. For all of the shortcomings that he may have possessed he decided to be a difference maker. At a time when the family experienced a maximum degree of uncertainty Monroe spoke these few words. "Can I help?"

In Monroe's hands was a money order in the amount of $1,000.00. I'm not sure who was more astonished me or my mother. For a brief period of time both of us stood in awe of what had just taken place. My mother seemed to stare endlessly at the money order in sheer disbelief. A gift of this magnitude from a family member who made very little money, considered a little slow, different, perhaps even retarded. What was it that had driven my brother to extend to me such a gift?

While we pondered this miraculous blessing Monroe left the room almost as quickly as he had appeared. He didn't see a need to hang around for any well deserved accolades.

Not knowing how to explain something seemingly unexplainable caused me to revert to my ghetto biblical philosophy. In other words not recalling the exact scriptures I combined my interpretation with what sounded good.

"Blessed are the least of thee when they share with someone else in need."

It sounded good to me. In addition I came to realize that in order for me or anyone to move on past something that was so difficult to grasp I had to find some closure.

After much consideration I decided that there was a safe, simplistic conclusion (ghetto biblical). Many are called, but few are chosen. Evidently I was the…chosen one!

www.ingramcontent.com/pod-product-compliance
Lightning Source LLC
LaVergne TN
LVHW051836080426
835512LV00018B/2908